Contents

Introduction

In this book we look at photographs and other kinds of images of prisons and the police force, from the 19th century up until the 1970s. We examine these images for clues about the past and see what we can learn from them about the way the solving of crimes and the treatment of prisoners has changed. On pages 30-31, you can find some questions and points to explore, to encourage further discussion of the pictures.

← This plan shows the layout of a prison.

↑ This is Dartmoor Prison. The prison was built in 1809. Britain was fighting France at the time, and it was originally built to house French prisoners of war. This plan shows the walls, prisoner accomodation, guard houses, hospital and other buildings.

4

→ **This document contains information about a young prisoner.**

→ Here we can find details about a young prisoner, George Page, aged 12. The document records that he was arrested for vagrancy (homelessness) and larceny (theft). He was sentenced to a month in prison followed by five years at a reformatory (reform school).

Lucy Freeman

← This is a photograph of a female prisoner.

← Victorian sentencing of female criminals could be harsh. One 19-year-old was sentenced to five years of hard labour for stealing an umbrella. Another received a similar sentence for stealing a rasher of bacon. If female prisoners were mothers of young children, the children were looked after in prison nurseries.

↓ **Newgate was a famous prison in London.**

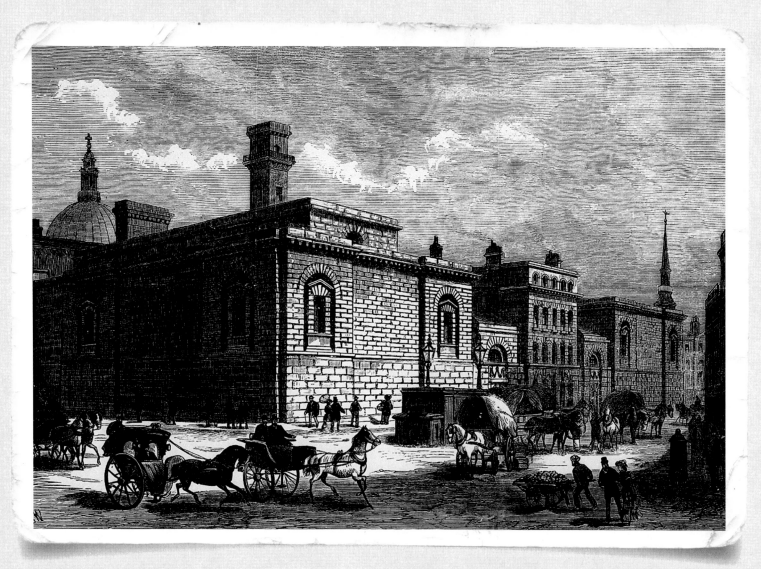

↑ The first Newgate Prison was built in 1188 and burned down in the Great Fire of London in 1666. The prison was rebuilt and, from 1783, it became the scene of many public hangings. The big dark platform in front of the prison is where the hangings used to take place.

⬇ **These convicts are exercising in the prison grounds.**

↑ In Victorian times, prisoners were kept on their own in their cells most of the time. When they were allowed out for exercise, they had to keep the same distance apart and were not allowed to talk to other prisoners.

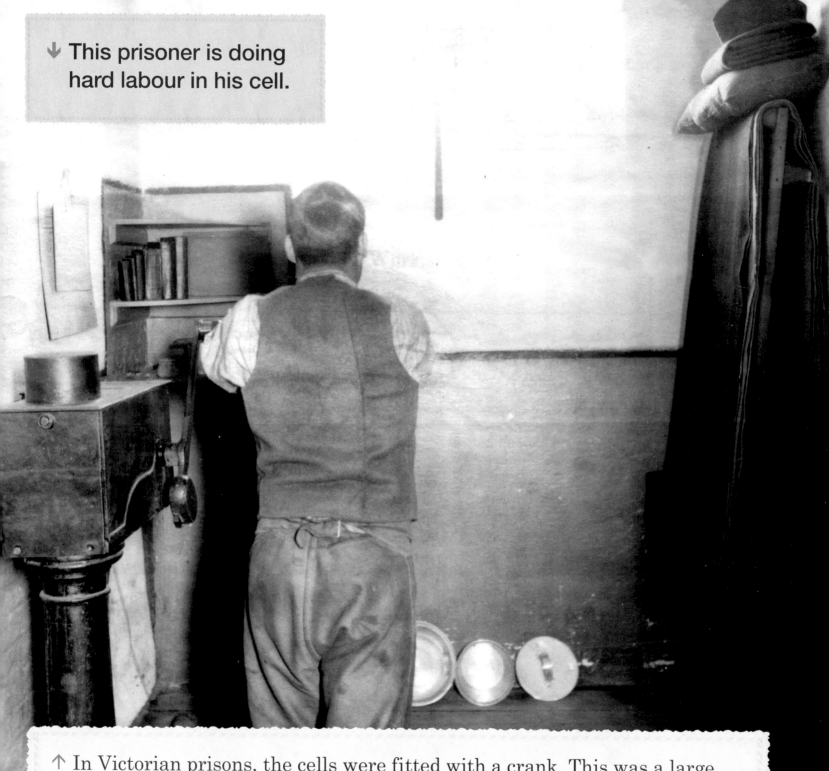

↓ This prisoner is doing hard labour in his cell.

↑ In Victorian prisons, the cells were fitted with a crank. This was a large handle fitted to a box with a counter. Prisoners had to do a certain number of turns each day to earn their food. Warders would tighten up the crank, making it harder to turn. This earned them the nickname 'screws'.

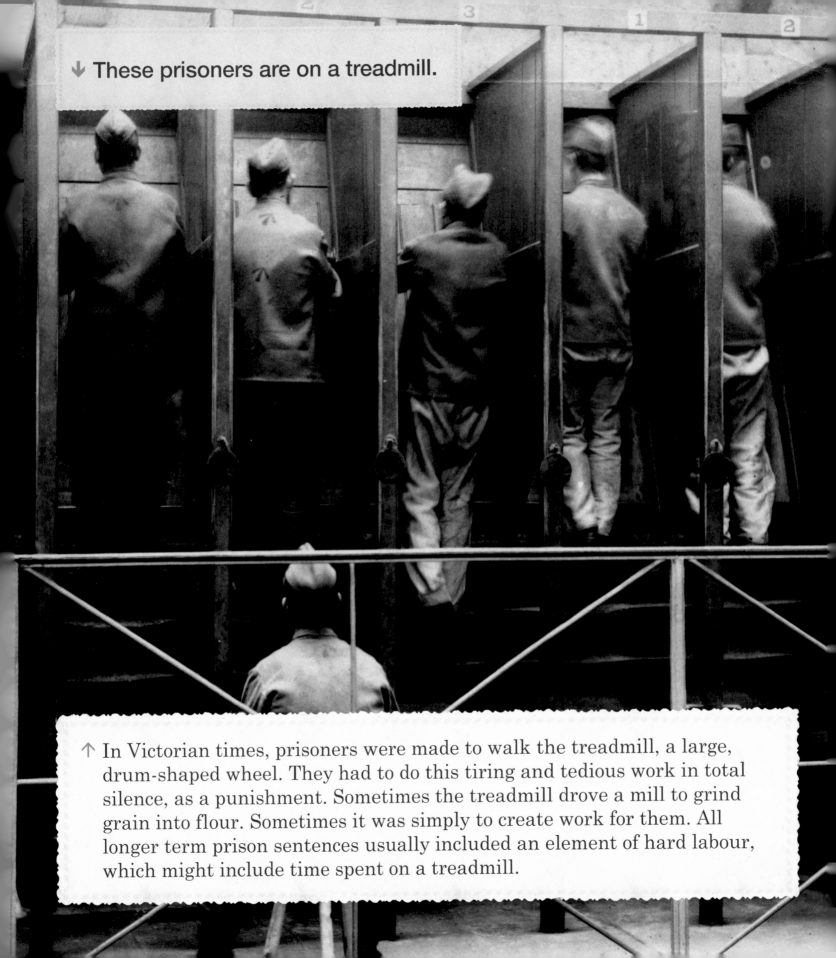

↓ These prisoners are on a treadmill.

↑ In Victorian times, prisoners were made to walk the treadmill, a large, drum-shaped wheel. They had to do this tiring and tedious work in total silence, as a punishment. Sometimes the treadmill drove a mill to grind grain into flour. Sometimes it was simply to create work for them. All longer term prison sentences usually included an element of hard labour, which might include time spent on a treadmill.

1895

↓ These men are handing out food to prisoners in their cells.

↑ Prison meals were very simple. They were usually bread and cocoa for breakfast, bread, meat, potatoes and soup for lunch, and bread and tea or gruel (oatmeal boiled in milk or water) for supper.

← These prisoners are making clothes.

↑ In the 19th century, the authorities believed it was important to set prisoners to work. This prison contained a tailor shop. Other prisons had woollen mills, shoemaking shops and farms. The products of these places were sold to make money for the prison. Prisoners were not paid for this work, and could be punished if they failed to reach their targets.

⬇ These female prisoners are scrubbing this walkway.

↑ All prisoners had to work very hard, including women. These women probably counted themselves lucky: the hardest labour was laundry work and twine making. The women who did these jobs received extra rations, including cheese for lunch.

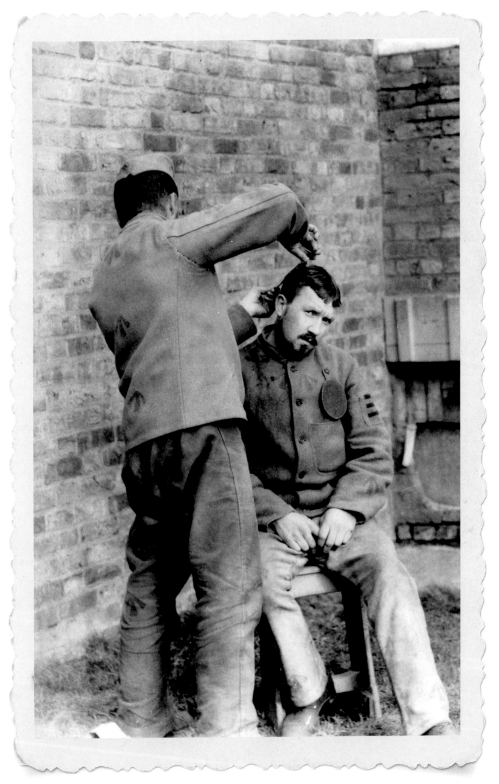

← This prisoner is having a haircut.

← On arrival at a Victorian prison, new convicts were given a cold bath and a haircut and were issued with a prison uniform. Everyone received the same short haircut.

↓ This is a prison kitchen. These men are about to prepare meals for the prisoners.

↑ In Victorian prisons, kitchen staff prepared individual meals for each prisoner. Food was cooked in the large vessels that lined the wall at the back of the kitchen, then placed in the small cans on the table. These were then put in the wooden trays and taken to the cells.

⬇ Ingredients are piled up on the table and the floor in this prison kitchen.

⬆ As a reward for good behaviour, some prisoners were allowed to work in the kitchens, preparing meals for other inmates. The job was not without hard work, however. Hauling around large sides of beef, for example, could be exhausting.

⬇ **These inmates have been made to face the wall while the prison rules are read to them.**

↑ Prisons were full of rules. There were rules for how often a male prisoner had to shave, how often they had to bathe, when clothes and bed linen had to be washed, when they could speak, eat, exercise and rest. Harsh punishments were handed out to those who broke the rules.

← This woman is a suffragette. She wants women to have the vote.

← Suffragettes did not regard themselves as criminals but as political campaigners, so they refused to stand still for mugshots. The police were forced to physically restrain them so their pictures could be taken. Even then, this suffragette, Evelyn Menesta, is pulling a face to make identification difficult. Suffragettes were often arrested for public order offences, and could be poorly treated in prison.

→ A police constable uses the telephone at a police box.

→ Police boxes were telephone boxes put in public places for the police to use, or for members of public to call the police. The telephone was placed behind a small, hinged door. The interior of the box was a miniature police station for the use of police officers. Police boxes first appeared in 1881 but are not used today because the police now use radios or mobile phones to communicate.

↓ These policemen are using motorcycles
with sidecars.

↑ The police have used motorcycles since the early 20th century. They use
them to patrol the streets enforcing traffic laws and to escort important
people. Motorcycles have advantages over other vehicles because they can
move at high speed through busy streets. They can catch speeding motorists
and reach accident scenes more quickly.

→ **This is the outside of Holloway Prison in London.**

→ Holloway Prison was built in 1852 in the style of a medieval castle, with turrets, battlements and arrow slits. It began as a mixed prison, but became female-only in 1903. Several suffragettes were imprisoned there.

1944

↓ This is a prison hospital. Prisoners go here if they get sick.

↑ Prisoners frequently suffered from health problems, due to poor diet, infection or addiction to alcohol or drugs. Prisons therefore needed to contain medical facilities, where prisoners could be treated. Prison hospitals needed to be secure too, though, to prevent prisoners from escaping.

⬇ These boys are inmates at a borstal. A borstal is a prison for young people.

⬆ Borstals were youth prisons that aimed to reform children found guilty of serious criminal behaviour. The first of these prisons was established in the village of Borstal in Kent in 1902. The emphasis was not on punishment, but on education, routine and discipline.

⬇ These policemen are responsible for crowd control at a football match.

↑ One job of the police is to control large crowds of people and prevent outbreaks of disorder and violence. This is especially important at football matches, where fights can sometimes occur between fans of rival teams, or at large political demonstrations, when people can feel very angry about a cause.

↓ Emergency calls to the police are received here.

↑ This is the information room at New Scotland Yard, the headquarters of the Metropolitan Police. Staff working here receive '999' calls. Police officers are then sent out to provide assistance when needed. Today, information room staff use computers to help make the process quicker and more accurate.

1967

← In the 1960s there were around 600 female police officers. Today there are around 35,000.

← The first female police officer, Sofia Stanley, was recruited to the Metropolitan Police in 1919. At first, female police officers' duties were quite limited. From 1937, they were allowed to take fingerprints. From 1946, married women could serve as police officers. Since 1973, female police officers have been paid the same amount as their male colleagues.

1960s

↓ New recruits at a police training school line up on parade.

↑ The first training school for police officers was founded in 1907 at Peel House in Pimlico. Recruits underwent a four-week course before being sent out on the beat. The new Peel House in Hendon, shown here, operated from 1934 until 1968, when building started on the Peel Centre. Today, the training course lasts 25 weeks.

↓ **This man is examining a car for evidence.**

↑ The police try to solve crimes by examining traces of evidence left at crime scenes. These can include blood, clothing fibres, tyre marks and fingerprints. Today, crime scene investigators (CSIs) dress very differently from the man in this picture. They wear special overalls, masks and gloves to avoid leaving any trace of their own bodies at the crime scene.

↓ **A police dog with its handler at Heathrow Airport.**

↑ Police dogs are used to detect illegal substances, such as explosives, to locate missing people and objects and to chase and hold suspects. They were first used in the UK in 1946. The first Alsatian was 'Smokey', who joined in 1948. A dog training school was set up in 1950. Today there are more 2,500 police dogs at work in the UK, and most regions have a police dog training school.

Questions to Ask and Points to Explore

Picture on page 4
Questions to ask
1. Why do you think the prison buildings were arranged in a circle?
2. Why do you think there are two walls and a fence around the prison?

Points to explore
Drawing: style and quality, handwriting, intention

Picture on page 5
Questions to ask
1. Do you think it is fair that this boy was sent to prison? Explain the reasons for your answer.
2. Give some possible reasons why George Page was homeless. Why do you think he committed larceny?

Points to explore
Photo: age, facial expression, clothing, sign, purpose
Document: handwriting, content (that can be deciphered)

Photograph on page 6
Questions to ask
1. Why do prison officials want a mugshot of every prisoner?
2. Why does the prisoner need to hold up a sign with her name on it?

Points to explore
Person: Gender, age, hairstyle, clothing, handwriting, facial expression

Picture on page 7
Questions to ask
1. Newgate Prison was designed to look ugly, with few windows and high stone walls. Why do you think this is?
2. Why do you think there is a tower rising above the main building?

Points to explore
Building: style of architecture, materials, fitness for purpose
Foreground: transport, clothing, depiction of street life

Photograph on page 8
Questions to ask
1. Why do you think the convicts are only walking on the paths?
2. Who do you think the man standing by the wall in the black uniform is?

3. Do you think the prisoners enjoyed this form of exercise?

Points to explore
Background: building design and materials, windows, towers
People: uniforms, activity

Photograph on page 9
Questions to ask
1. Why do you think the prisoners were forced to turn the crank?
2. The wooden object leaning against the wall is the prisoner's bed. Do you think the prisoner was comfortable in this cell?

Points to explore
Background: bed, cushions, stool, crank, pots and pans, books, walls, décor
Person: clothing

Photograph on page 10
Questions to ask
1. Why do you think the men have been separated into compartments?
2. What do you think the little circular objects hanging on hooks behind each prisoner are? For a clue, look at the picture on page 11.

Points to explore
Background: treadmill structure, materials
People: uniforms, activity

Photograph on page 11
Questions to ask
1. Who are the men in black with the peak caps?
2. Why are the prisoners wearing badges?

Points to explore
Background: cell doorways, walls, style of paintwork, tray of food
People: uniforms, facial expressions, badges

Photograph on page 12
Questions to ask
1. Why do you think prison authorities believed it was important for prisoners to work?
2. Some prisoners stole the coats they made in the tailor shop. Can you think why?

Points to explore
Room: décor, furniture, equipment
People: uniforms, activities, facial expressions, light

Photograph on page 13
Questions to ask
1. Why do you think the prison authorities employed prisoners to clean and maintain the buildings?
2. Women rose at six o'clock and spent much of their day doing physical work, with breaks for eating, going to chapel and exercise. What do you think about their lives? What do you think they might have missed?

Points to explore
Background: walkway, buckets, soap
People: gender, uniform, activity, behaviour

Photograph on page 14
Questions to ask
1. Why do you think the prison authorities wanted prisoners to have short hair?
2. Look carefully at the man giving the haircut. Do you think he's a prisoner or a warder? Why do you think this?

Points to explore
Background: grass, brickwork
People: uniform, hairstyle, facial expressions

Photograph on page 15
Questions to ask
1. What clues does this picture give us that this kitchen is set up to serve a large number of people?
2. Where will the ingredients be chopped and prepared? Where will the food be cooked?

Points to explore
Room: size, materials, windows, light, furniture, equipment, containers
People: clothing, hairstyles, facial expressions

Photograph on page 16
Questions to ask
1. How does this kitchen differ from, say, one found in a large stately home?
2. Why do you think prison meals were very simple and the same each day?

Points to explore
Room: materials, cooking equipment, food, cans, fireplace, food
People: clothing, activity

Photograph on page 17
Questions to ask
1. Why do you think the prisoners have been

made to face the wall while the rules are being read out to them?

2. Why did prisons have so many rules?

3. What does this say about what the prison authorities thought about the prisoners?

Points to explore

Background: pillars, walkway, atmosphere
People: uniforms, activity, attitude

Picture on page 18

Questions to ask

1. Do you think suffragettes were right to try to avoid having their photos taken?

2. The police later published a photo of Evelyn Menesta with the restraining arm removed from her neck. Why do you think they did this?

3. Do you think the suffragettes were right to break the law as part of their campaign to win the right to vote?

Points to explore

Background: brickwork, barred gate
People: clothing, gender, facial expression, restraining arm

Photograph on page 19

Questions to ask

1. In what famous television series does a police box regularly appear?

2. Why do you hardly ever see police boxes today?

Points to explore

Background: hinged door, old-fashioned telephone, wire, missing window panes
Person: uniform, pose, gender

Photograph on page 20

Questions to ask

1. Why do the police use motorcycles?

2. What do you think the men in the sidecars are holding to their ears?

3. How do these motorcycle riders' outfits differ from modern motorcyclists? Why do you think riding motorcycles in those days might have been dangerous?

Points to explore

Building: design and materials, age

Photograph on page 21

Questions to ask

1. Why do you think there is netting placed in the central space between the upper walkways?

2. Do you think it's right that prison hospitals should be high security? Should prisoners be kept in handcuffs while they are receiving medical treatment?

Points to explore

Building: design, materials, furniture, walkways, steps, doorways and windows

Photograph on page 22

Questions to ask

1. Why do you think the architects decided to design this prison to look like a castle?

2. Five women were executed at Holloway Prison between 1903 and 1955, including the last woman to be hanged in Britain. Can you find out her name?

Points to explore

Building: design and materials, age

Photograph on page 23

Questions to ask

1. These are inmates of Feltham Borstal in south-west London. Do you agree with the idea that young offenders should be locked up?

2. The boys are returning from a day's work outside the prison. Can you tell from their tools the sort of work they have been doing?

Points to explore

Background: building and wall design and materials, trees
People: age, clothing, uniforms, style of movement

Picture on page 24

Questions to ask

1. There is a policeman on horseback in this photo. Why might mounted police be useful in crowd control? What qualities must the horse have?

2. Who do you think the man speaking to the row of policemen is? What might he be saying to the men? What sort of problems do you think might occur during a football match?

Points to explore

Background: football stadium stand, turnstiles, signs, football club emblem on wall

People: gender; uniforms, whistle, lack of protective equipment, facial expressions

Photograph on page 25

Questions to ask

1. How does this differ from a modern office? There is a clock in the room, and a calendar. Why do you think knowing the time and date is so important for the people working here?

2. There is a map of London in the corner. What do you think this is used for?

Points to explore

Background: furniture, charts, equipment
People: gender, uniforms, activities

Photograph on page 26

Questions to ask

1.What are some of the differences between the male and female uniforms?

2. Do you think the 1967 uniform is practical and authoritative? Can you think of ways it might be improved?

Points to explore

Background: New Scotland Yard sign, building
Person: pose, expression, uniform

Photograph on page 27

Questions to ask

1. Think about all the jobs the police have to do. Now draw up a list of subjects that you think need to be covered during a police training course.

Points to explore

Background: parade ground
People: stance, uniforms, gender

Photograph on page 28

Questions to ask

1. This car might have been stolen, or used by robbers to get away from a bank. What do you think the police officer is looking for on the window, and how will this help him solve the crime?

2. The car is part of a crime scene. Signs are put up around the vehicle to keep people away. Why is it important that members of the public don't enter a crime scene?

Points to explore

Background: old-fashioned car
Person: gender, equipment, clothing, hairstyle

Photograph on page 29

Questions to ask

1. Why do you think dogs are useful to the police? What can dogs do better than humans and how might this be helpful?

2. The Metropolitan Police now has its own police dog breeding programme, supplying the UK and the world with police dogs. Write a list of the special qualities you think a police dog should have.

Points to explore

Background: aeroplane, car, runway
Person: uniform, gender, hairstyle
Dog: breed, alertness, leash

Some suggested answers can be found on the Wayland website www.waylandbooks.co.uk.

Further Information

Books

Crime and Punishment *(Twentieth Century Issues)* by Alison Brownlie (Wayland, 1999)
Prison and the Penal System *(Criminal Justice)* by Michael Newton (Chelsea House, 2010)
Prisons and Prisoners *(Painful History of Crime)* by John Townsend (Raintree, 2005)
Victorian Crime *(Be A History Detective)* by Liz Gogerly (Wayland, 2009)
Victorian Crime *(Victorian Britain)* by Fiona MacDonald (Franklin Watts, 2009)

Websites

http://vcp.e2bn.org/gaols/index.php
http://www.nationalarchives.gov.uk/education/lesson24.htm
http://writingwomenshistory.blogspot.co.uk/2010/08/daily-life-in-victorian-womens-prison.html
http://www.victorianlondon.org/prisons/wormwood.htm
http://www.bl.uk/learning/histcitizen/victorians/crime/prisongallery/victorianprisons.html

Glossary

architect A person who designs buildings.

breakwater A barrier built out into a body of water to protect a coast or harbour from the force of the waves.

campaign To work in an organised and active way towards a particular goal.

Central Criminal Court The court, based in London, that deals with the major criminal cases of England and Wales. It is more commonly known as the Old Bailey.

chaplain A member of the clergy attached to an institution such as a prison.

convict A person found guilty of a criminal offence who is serving a prison sentence.

custody Imprisonment.

decipher To convert text written in code into normal language.

demolished (of a building) Knocked down.

gallows A structure, usually made up of two uprights and a crosspiece, for the hanging of criminals.

hard labour Heavy work given to convicts as a punishment.

identification The process of working out who someone is.

inmate A person confined to a prison or a prison hospital.

larceny Theft.

layout The way in which the parts of something are arranged or laid out.

mill Machinery for grinding grain into flour.

mugshot A photograph of a person's face made for an official purpose, particularly for police records.

public order offence A crime, such as the destruction of property, that interferes with the normal running of society.

rations A fixed amount of something, such as food, that each person is allowed.

reform school A place where young offenders were sent instead of prison.

secure (of an institution) Built and guarded to make it harder for inmates to escape.

sentence The punishment given to someone found guilty by a court.

side of beef Either the left or right half of the body of a cow prepared for eating.

suffragette A woman seeking the right to vote through organised protest.

tailor shop A workshop where clothes are made.

tedious Boring.

twine Strong thread or string made of strands of hemp, cotton or nylon twisted together.

warder A guard in a prison.